# Spotlight on Colorado

# THE ECONOMY OF COLORADO

Heather Niver

PowerKiDS press™

NEW YORK

Published in 2016 by The Rosen Publishing Group, Inc.
29 East 21st Street, New York, NY 10010

Book Design: Iron Cupcake Design

Cataloging-in-Publication Data

Names: Niver, Heather.
Title: The economy of Colorado / Heather Niver.
Description: New York : PowerKids Press, 2016. | Series: Spotlight on Colorado | Includes index.
Identifiers: ISBN 9781499415063 (pbk.) | ISBN 9781499415094 (6 pack) | ISBN 9781499415117 (library bound)
Subjects: LCSH: Colorado--Juvenile literature. | Colorado--Economic conditions--Juvenile literature. | Classification: LCC F776.3 N58 2016 | DDC 978.8--dc23

Photo Credits: fFooter/Shutterstock.com, cover; Images by Dr. Alan Lipkin/Shutterstock.com, 3; Arina P Habich /Shutterstock.com, 5; T Cassidy/Shutterstock.com, 5; welcomia/Shutterstock.com, 7; Lilac Mountain/Shutterstock.com, 8; wavebreakmedia/Shutterstock.com, 9; Arina P Habich/ Shutterstock.com, 11; farbled/Shutterstock.com, 12; marekuliasz/Shutterstock.com, 13; LC-DIG-ppmsca-18007/loc.gov, 15; AP Photo/File, 16; Jim Lambert/Shutterstock.com, 17; Arina P Habich/Shutterstock.com, 18; Arina P Habich /Shutterstock.com, 19; AP Photo/Ed Andrieski, 21; MARK LEFFINGWELL/AFP/Getty Images, 23; John Moore/Getty Images, 25; AP Photo/The Montrose Daily Press, Eric Drummond, 27; AP Photo/Brennan Linsley, 29; rCarner/Shutterstock.com, 31; rCarner/Shutterstock.com, 32; Arina P Habich/Shutterstock.com, 33; Vladislav Gajic/Shutterstock. com, 34; Zack Frank/Shutterstock.com, 35; Chad Bontrager/Shutterstock.com, 36; Phillip Rubino/ Shutterstock.com, 37; RDaniel/Shutterstock.com, 39; Vicki L. Miller/Shutterstock.com, 41; John Moore/ Getty Images, 42; Arina P Habich/Shutterstock.com, 43; Arina P Habich/Shutterstock.com, 45.

Manufactured in the United States of America

CPSIA Compliance Information: Batch #BW16PK: For further information contact Rosen Publishing, New York, New York at 1-800-237-9932

# Contents

# CHAPTER 1

# More Moolah: Money Matters

## KINDS OF CAPITAL

Capital refers to wealth, which can mean money or assets. Each person's individual, personal income in a certain area is known as per capita income. There is also total state product, or gross state product. This is a measurement how much the state produces. Total state product is figured by adding up the value from all the industries all over the state.

Colorado is known as a great place to live and visit, but its economy is what keeps it running. A big part of Colorado's economy is supported by mining and agriculture. But what does that mean? An economy is the part of a society that builds wealth, or makes money. Wealth is more than money, like dollars and cents. Wealth can be the result of making goods and services. People use their money to buy goods and services. Goods are objects, like fruit orchards, livestock, and even highways and roads. Services are things people do for each other. Services can include teaching skiing lessons or taking care of someone's health, like a doctor. People who use goods and services are called consumers.

Someone needs to create the goods that people buy. That process is known as **production**. There are three parts to production. The first part is land. Land can

Colorado's economy is made up of a wide variety of goods and services. These include fruit orchards, health care, energy, mining, tourism, skiing, farming, and livestock.

*Fort Collins, Colorado, began as an agricultural town. Today, it has many industries, but growing crops is still one of them.*

mean a sprawling farm, a small business, or a workshop. It can also refer to **natural resources**, which are things that are a part of nature. Examples are oil, water, and minerals. Second, is labor, or the workers. Workers are paid for their work with wages. The third part of production is **capital**. Capital resources are things like the tools, factories, and offices that all work together to create goods and services.

## COLORADO AND OUR COUNTRY'S COINS

There are only three places where our country's coins are created. Denver, Colorado, is one of the three U.S. Mints! Each coin has a letter, or mintmark. The mintmark shows where the coins are made. So when you see a letter D on a coin with a date after 1906, that means it was made in Denver!

# CHAPTER 2

# How Geography Affects Economy

Oh, the mountains! Those gorgeous, snowy peaks are one of the first things to come to mind when people think about Colorado. The state's geography is truly unforgettable.

These breathtaking views also help support Colorado's economy. Colorado is home to four national parks, as well as many national monuments, state parks, and historic sites. These include Rocky Mountain National Park and Mesa Verde National Park. In addition, Colorado has many ski resort towns that attract skiers from around the globe. Colorado also has many events each year, such as rodeos, film festivals, and art and food festivals. These, too, attract many tourists and visitors to the state.

Tourism and recreation make a lot of money for the state. Think about how much **revenue** tourists can bring in. Visitors buy souvenirs

*Today, Breckenridge is known for its many ski resorts.*

to remember the trip, eat out at restaurants, stay in hotels, and visit attractions. This makes money for the state. It also creates jobs, as people work in these hotels, restaurants, and ski resorts. Colorado can boast getting 26 million visitors every year! And all these people bring in more than $7 billion a year.

Tourism is great for the economy. All those visitors are not so great for the wildlife. And that's what many tourists flock to the state to see. Resorts and other visitor's centers get bigger. But they use up more and more of that wild space. In some places, too many wood-burning stoves cause pollution. It has gotten so bad that the government has to limit new fireplaces in new homes!

There are three mines in Colorado that still produce gold. The biggest is the Cripple Creek & Victor Gold Mine.

OIL PUMPJACK

*Oil is a natural resource found in Colorado.*

Without the income it makes from tourism, Colorado might be a very poor state. But tourism is not the only way that Colorado's geography and natural resources benefit its economy. Colorado's other **industries** include minerals and energy. Its main mineral wealth comes from a few natural resources. They include minerals like gold and coal. However, neither minerals nor energy brings in as much revenue as tourism.

Another surprising benefit to Colorado's economy comes from its time zone. Denver is located in the west-central Mountain Time Zone. This location comes in handy for the **telecommunications** industry. Why? Because Denver is smack in the middle of the country. The United States is an enormous country. So this position is handy. This time zone allows businesses to communicate with both North American coasts in the same business day. They can contact South America, Europe, and Asia, too!

*Telecommunications is one of several industries that keep Colorado's modern economy thriving.*

# CHAPTER 3

# Natural Resources, Power, and Energy

Naturally occurring features are called natural resources. Examples of natural resources include things like forests, water, minerals, and land. They can be used to create money and wealth. Some natural resources can also create power—power that can be used to drive cars, provide electricity and heat, and run factories.

Having its own sources of power is good for a big state like Colorado. It saves and even makes them money. For years, coal was the state's main source of power. Colorado has some of the richest sources of coal in the United States. These coal sources are found in the northwest area of the state. Today, Colorado still depends on coal. But it relies more heavily on renewable sources.

WRANGLE UP SOME FACTS

Colorado gets 13.6 percent of its in-state electricity needs from wind power.

*Wind turbines, like these in Limon, Colorado, produce renewable energy for the state.*

Wind is one renewable natural resource. Power can be created from wind using wind turbines. Colorado wind power has become very important since 2000. Today, it makes up most generated power. And this electricity doesn't create any pollution!

## HOT STUFF!

Another renewable source of power is called geothermal energy. This is energy created from the Earth's heat. It uses heat from underground steam. In 2013, the Colorado State Capitol building became the first to be kept cool using geothermal energy. It is the first capitol building in the U.S. to enjoy geothermal cooling on hot summer days.

Mining has been an important part of Colorado's economy since the 19th century. In fact, gold and silver mining led to Colorado's population growing very quickly in the late 1800s, which in turn helped it to become a state. Today, mining still makes up a big part of the state's income. Colorado is the fourth-largest gold producing state in the United States. Coal is also mined in Colorado, with eleven active mines located in the western part of the state.

MOLYBDENUM

Besides gold and coal, some of the state's main minerals include **petroleum** (an oily liquid used in fuels), **molybdenum** (a metal used in steel), and plain old sand and gravel.

## FRACKING

Oil shales became a new energy resource after the year 2000. Shale is a soft rock that can be split easily. Some shale contains oil. Oil and gas have been removed from the rock with water. This process of removing the oil from the shale is called fracking. This oil can be used as energy. Not everyone is a fan of fracking. They argue that fracking is not good for the environment. Some of the water used in fracking may contain harmful chemicals. Scientists continue to study the effects of fracking. Their work will help decide if fracking is a good enough source of energy to outweigh the environmental harm.

*Idylwilde is a dam on the Big Thompson River that produces hydroelectric power.*

**Hydroelectric** power also helps keep Colorado moving. This electricity is created using the motion of water. Hydroelectric power also makes money for the city of Boulder. They can sell some of that electricity. In 2013, the selling of hydroelectric power brought in $1.9 million.

## NUCLEAR WEAPONS
The Rocky Flats weapons plant is near Denver. It used to make nuclear weapons. However, making nuclear weapons caused dangerous pollution, and the plant was shut down.

# CHAPTER 4

# Changing Times, Changing Economy

Colorado officially became a state on August 1, 1876. Of course it didn't draw in the crowds of tourists (and their money) to the ski slopes back then. But it was its natural resources that first attracted visitors to the state. When people got wind of gold in an area, they rushed there to make their fortunes. Colorado was no exception. For its first century, mining gold and silver was the state's main economic industry. These resources led to jobs not just for miners. The miners needed goods and services, which led to new businesses like hotels, restaurants, and general stores.

## MANY NICKNAMES

Colorado has not one, but six nicknames! It's called the Centennial State because it became a state 100 years after the Declaration of Independence was signed. It's called the Silver State and also the Lead State. Silver and lead were both mined here. So many bison (once called buffalo) used to roam here that it is called the Buffalo State. It's called the Highest State because of its high mountain peaks. And finally, it's called the Switzerland of America. This name comes from the state's amazing natural beauty and mountains, like those found in Switzerland.

*Silverton, seen here, was, as its name suggests, one of Colorado's silver mining boomtowns.*

But after the 1880s, things began to change. Many of the top-producing gold mines were running dry. Also, the government began buying less silver, which caused demand for silver to decline. Still, through World War II in the first half of the 20th century, Colorado remained dependent on the state's natural resources. Agriculture and mining were the economy's main muscle.

## PIKES PEAK OR BUST!

In 1806, Lieutenant Zebulon Pike found a mountain in Colorado. It was later named for him. Gold was found in the area in 1858. The notable peak was used as a landmark for travelers during the gold rush. Those in search of fortune would write "Pikes Peak or Bust" on their wagons.

These days, Colorado is home to five air force bases and two army bases.

*This 1940 photograph shows a bomber at Lowry Air Force Base in Colorado. The base closed in 1994.*

During and after World War II, the federal government focused on expanding its defense facilities in Colorado. This brought new industry and money to the state. It included the building of military facilities like the Lowry Air Force Base near Denver. This was used for training the air force during World War II and beyond. Fort Carson in Colorado Springs was another army installation. It was built in 1942 and is still used today. In the 1960s, cuts to defense spending caused another shift. After this point, technology and service industries began to power Colorado's economy.

The 1980s saw a nasty economic downturn. After slow growth, by 1990, economic strength began to return. Colorado's new economic growth occurred in the areas of advanced technology and construction. Telecommunications was a huge benefit to Colorado's economy. This economic upward swing peaked in 2000. After that, it began to decline as the whole country experienced a **recession**. Colorado was slow to bounce back compared to the rest of the United States.

Today, the state is a huge tourist destination. Energy production and medical technology are also big economic contributors.

FORT CARSON

## THEY SAID NO!

In 1972, Colorado was made an offer most states would not refuse. They had the chance to host the 1976 Olympic Games! But the voters had other ideas. They objected to holding the games in their state. They voted no. They felt that Colorado should not use tax money to fund this huge project. Colorado is the only state to refuse an invitation to host the Olympics.

# CHAPTER 5

# Today's Labor Force

By 2013, Colorado was one of only 13 states to fully recover from a recent recession. In fact, its employment was growing. Colorado had the third-fastest employment growth rate in the country. (It was sixth in 2012.) In 2014, employment was increasing and reached a state high not seen since 2000. Its workforce increased by 70,700 jobs in 2014. Out of

*University of Colorado at Colorado Springs*

Colorado's total population of 5.3 million people, 2.3 million were working that year. Both national and global businesses succeed in Colorado.

Today, Colorado is known for having a talented workforce. It is also a very well-educated workforce. Almost 38 percent of the population is younger than age 25 and has a bachelor's degree. And its growing economy has that well-informed group to thank. It's also a young workforce. Ten percent is made up of **millennials**, or those born in the 1980s and 1990s. A young, talented workforce helps keep the economy in good shape.

If it continues at its current growth rates, Colorado's population is expected to reach 6 million by 2020.

*Denver is a major metropolitan city, and its workforce includes many young professionals.*

"[Colorado's economy] is ranking in the top five nationally for population growth, employment growth, wage and salary growth, and personal income growth."
—Economist Richard Wobbekind of University of Colorado's Leeds School of Business

Lots of talented people live in Colorado and start businesses there. Colorado is home to many **entrepreneurs**, innovations, and start-up businesses. Entrepreneurs do well in Colorado because they get a lot of support. For example, the state offers them financial help. They employ people with talents in the science and research fields. Colorado is fourth in the nation for the number of **sole proprietors**, or people who are the exclusive owner of their business, living there.

Colorado is a good place for businesses to make their roots. The state's tax structure makes it a positive place to make investments and start new ground-breaking businesses. Taxes are a percent of money that businesses and individuals pay to the government. Colorado businesses don't have to pay superhigh corporate taxes, either. In fact, Colorado's tax rate (4.63 percent) is the lowest in the country. So it's called a pretty tax-friendly state. Colorado also stays hands-off as far as regulating businesses, compared to other states, too. No wonder businesses want to make Colorado their home!

Congratulations, Colorado! According to *Business Insider*, Colorado has the top economy in the country.

The popular tea maker Celestial Seasons has a plant in Boulder, Colorado. The company was founded in 1969.

# CHAPTER 6

# The Federal Government

Colorado has its own government. So do each of the other 49 states in the United States. The federal government is also called the national government. Some of its powers extend to the whole country. But each state has its own rules and regulations, too. The U.S. Constitution is a document that makes sure that the state and federal government have balanced powers.

Colorado is home to lots of federal agencies, or organizations. In fact, the Denver-Aurora metropolitan area has more federal workers than any other area except Washington, D.C. About 37 percent of Colorado is made up of national forests. This land belongs to the federal government. It takes a lot of people to keep that land ready for visitors.

Government agencies might sound like boring businesses. Not so! One branch of NORAD (North American Aerospace Defense Command) is located near Colorado Springs.

## WHAT'S THE WEATHER?

The Earth System Research Laboratory of NOAA, or the National Oceanic and Atmospheric Administration, is located in Boulder. They do a lot of exciting work there. Their scientists study atmospheric and other processes that affect air quality, weather, and climate. By doing that, they can better understand daily weather, severe storms such as hurricanes, and climate in the decades to come.

**NORTH AMERICAN AEROSPACE DEFENSE COMMAND (NORAD) IN COLORADO SPRINGS**

It is a government organization that works with Canada. They control **aerospace** and deal with any related warnings, like attacks. NORAD is basically in charge of our airspace. Keeping track of our airspace is one of the most important parts of our defense system. So NORAD is not out in the open. In Colorado Springs you'll find a site of mystery and secrecy: Cheyenne Mountain Complex. Inside a mountain, NORAD keeps its top-secret information.

## KEEP IT SECRET, KEEP IT SAFE
Cheyenne Mountain Complex is a top-secret spot. Only those with the highest security clearance can go there. It is a hollow mountain full of caves. It even has an underground lake! Cheyenne Mountain is the home to the country's most important data and information.

# Wealth and Poverty

Magazines are full of glossy photos of grinning skiers rushing down Colorado's mountains. There is talk in the news about funky new start-up businesses in the cities and towns. Such images might make it seem like Colorado is one big wealthy state.

But not all Colorado is made up of happy hiking tourists. Like any state, Colorado has its share of poorer people, too. Poverty means being extremely poor. In Colorado, more than one out of every eight people lived in poverty in 2013. The number is worse for kids. One in six lived in poverty. That same year, one out of seven people did not have enough money to feed their families. People fall into these troubling situations in all kinds of ways. Some lose their jobs, for example. Others might be too ill to work or have other health problems.

Poverty can be caused by all kinds of things. For example, sometimes people live in areas

*These people are volunteering on Thanksgiving to give a hot meal to those in need.*

where the schools are not very good. Poor schools makes it less likely that kids will go on to college and from there get good jobs. Some areas with high poverty might not have any jobs for people. Or they might have a limited number of jobs, but these jobs might not pay very well. A low-paying job makes it harder for a family to make ends meet.

## COLORADO'S POOR

Otero County is located in the southeastern corner of the state. It is the poorest area in Colorado. Between 2009 and 2013, the average income for a household was only $33,848. The county's unemployment rate is more than double that of the state average. It was 8.8 percent in 2013. From 2009 to 2013, only about 15.5 percent of people in the county went on to get a 4-year college degree. Compare that to the state rate of 28.8 percent. And remember that Colorado is known for its well-educated residents.

# CHAPTER 8

# Industries

Colorado is a state that many industries call home. An industry is a business that provides a specific good or service. Food processing, transportation equipment, and military weaponry are just a few industries that keep Colorado's economy humming. Food processing means taking raw ingredients and creating food that can be sold to people to eat. Food processing companies in Colorado include Leprino Foods, the largest producer of mozzarella cheese in the world, and JBS USA, the U.S. headquarters of the largest meat-packing company in the world.

Some of the big brands you see on store shelves all over the country are made in Colorado. Those sweet fruity candies known as Jolly Ranchers were made by Bill and Dorothy Harmsen. Their factory was a red-and-white striped barn in Wheat Ridge, Colorado. (Hershey bought it in 1997. In 2002, it moved the

## WHAT'S BREWING?

Colorado now also has the largest annual production of beer of any state. Craft, or handmade, breweries are popping up everywhere in the state. Small craft breweries add products and jobs. They also draw in tourists who enjoy touring different breweries. Many breweries have tasting rooms where visitors who are of legal drinking age can get a sampling of the various beers made there. With 150 breweries across the state, beer-lovers can keep pretty busy.

Other brands you might recognize have their roots in Colorado: Celestial Seasonings tea is based in Boulder, and Samsonite luggage was founded in Denver.

*Russell Stover Candies has a factory in the town of Montrose, Colorado. For chocolate lovers, it might be a fun place to work!*

Colorado factory to California.) But don't worry. Colorado still has its fair share of sweet treats. Russell Stover Candies makes its chocolate confections in Montrose.

Two other major types of business in this state are the scientific research and high-technology industries. For example, aerospace depends on research to continually develop and improve their technologies.

## MARIJUANA

In 2014, Colorado's Amendment 64 made it legal to sell marijuana, or cannabis, in Colorado. It is legal for adults 21 and older to buy it. In 2014, its sales reached $700 million. If sales continue at this rate, by 2016 that number might be $1 billion! That's a significant boost to the economy!

Computers and other technological equipment are the main kinds of machinery made in Colorado. In fact, there are a few communities in the Front Range, the area east of the Rocky Mountains, that have created special manufacturing parks. Here they only make products like semiconductors, which are solid elements that help conduct electricity. Many electronics depend on them to work. Businesses in these manufacturing parks make parts that are important in computers and robotics.

The electronics industry is also big in Colorado. It makes electronics, parts used to make them, and provides services. Colorado manufactures Earth-friendly lighting that can be made without using too many natural resources. It also makes special sensors that are necessary for electronics used in space. Arrow Electronics makes 40 percent of the world's electronics. It makes more money for the state than any other company in Colorado. The aerospace, bioscience, defense manufacturing, and technology industries all need electronics to do their work.

In 2010, the National Aeronautics and Space Administration (NASA) gave $1.5 billion in contracts to Colorado aerospace companies.

Colorado ranks second in the United States for the number of jobs in the private-sector aerospace industry.

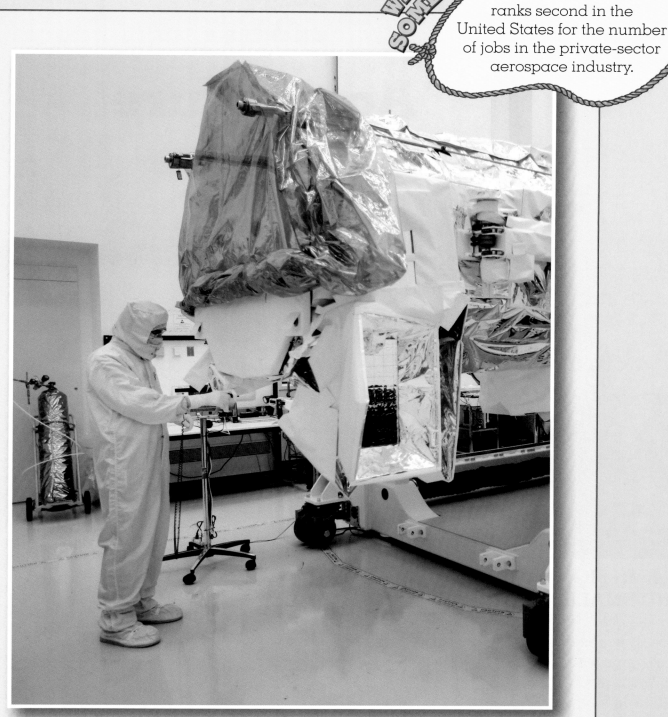

*Here, a technician works on a high-resolution imaging satellite for the company Ball Aerospace in Boulder, Colorado.*

# CHAPTER 9

# Agriculture

Agriculture and food production are another major part of Colorado's economy. This includes farming, ranching, organic foods, craft beverages, and even worldwide restaurant companies. In fact, these industries contribute a whopping $5 billion every year to the state's economy. These industries also add jobs for 173,000 people. Agriculture is a powerful part of the state's economy. Governor John Hickenlooper feels that, together with the food industry, agriculture helped move Colorado out of a recession. Colorado exports food to more than 100 countries.

Raising cattle is the biggest source of farm income. Its contribution is 60 percent, in fact. This mostly comes from cattle and calves. Colorado's other top agricultural products are dairy products. Colorado's cows make more milk per cow than anywhere else in the

## FARMS BIG AND SMALL

Farms come in all sizes. They can be small gardens to enormous ranches that go on for miles and miles.

Some ranches are also tourist attractions. People can come and stay on working ranches and learn what it's like to be a cowboy.

CATTLE

country. Colorado is one of the top ten cattle producing states in the United States. Sheep are also raised in Colorado. Chickens are raised for their eggs.

## HAPPY COWS

With all those animals raised for their meat and for their milk, you may wonder how they are treated. Colorado is a leader in animal welfare, or their health and happiness. They take care of the animals that give them so much.

*Siphon tubes, seen here, help irrigate crops in Colorado's semiarid climate.*

Colorado has a climate that is semiarid (dry) and sunny. But crops and animals need their water! Colorado does not get much rainfall. Agriculture uses a lot of the state's water. In Colorado, if a river or stream runs through or along your farm or property, you can use that water. (That does not mean you own it.) Colorado was the first state to treat water this way.

The soils in the eastern part of the state are very fertile. This helps many crops to grow. Colorado also produces corn for grain and greenhouse and nursery products (especially carnations).

As for fruit, apples are the top crop here. Large orchards are found on the Western Slope and in the Rio Grande valley in southern Colorado. Vineyards are also an economic benefit. Colorado has two areas where wine is produced, which adds to the economy. Tourists enjoy visiting vineyards and wineries, just as they visit craft breweries.

Additional important agricultural products include wheat, hay, beans, potatoes, cantaloupe, lettuce, sweet corn, and sugar beets. Sugar beets are a natural source of sugar.

**OH, THE WATER**
Colorado has special tunnels, called diversion tunnels, to move water where it is needed.

*Colorado is also home to vineyards, such as this one in Palisade.*

# CHAPTER 10

# Tourism

Summer, winter, spring, or fall. Colorado's tourism industry seems to be popular all year round. In 2011, 57.9 million people visited. The year before, they spent more than $14 billion during their visits. The year 2013 was record setting. That number had spiked to more than 64 million visitors. They spent more than $17 billion. In 2013, the state provided 150,700 jobs in tourism. These employees earned about $4.7 billion that year.

Outdoor activities are obviously a huge part of the state's income. The most important areas include Vail, Aspen, Steamboat Springs, and Breckenridge. Four national parks draw in the tourists. These are Rocky Mountain, Black Canyon of the Gunnison, Great Sand Dunes, and Mesa Verde. Together, they make up a huge part of the state: 710 square miles (1,840 sq km). Outdoor events like Alpine World Ski Championships draw people, too.

Mesa Verde National Park is most well-known for its cliff dwellings, which were made by some of Colorado's earliest inhabitants. The Ancestral Pueblo people lived here from AD 600 to 1300.

A Colorado tourism motto is "Come to Life" in Colorado.

GREAT SAND DUNES NATIONAL PARK

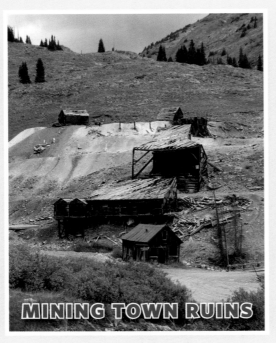
MINING TOWN RUINS

Tourists don't only come to Colorado for its peaks and trails. They visit many historic places and eat delicious foods. Some visitors come to learn about Colorado's rich history, including its ghost towns. What is a ghost town? They start out as boomtowns. Boomtowns spring up when an area experiences very rapid growth and wealth. For example, new communities popped up where there was gold during the gold rush. In some cases, after the excitement of gold died down, the people went to live in other places. A ghost town was left behind. Those who are up for an adventure of a different kind can go visit the old ghost towns. Some cool Colorado towns offer eerie, quiet tours of their quiet old streets. Others towns continued to thrive and are now popular tourist destinations, such as ski resorts. Examples include Breckenridge, Leadville, and Idaho Springs.

Tourists who want to appreciate Colorado's history while also enjoying its beautiful scenery can take a ride on a historic railroad through the mountains.

*Thrill seekers can enjoy white-water rafting just 30 minutes from Denver on the Clear Creek River.*

Others enjoy exploring the state's ecotourism, which is discovering threatened or conserved natural areas. These trips are usually organized so that the tours do not damage or harm the areas in any way. The tours may even benefit or sustain the areas. Another unusual tourism draw for Colorado is agritourism, which involves visiting and even working on a farm.

## BUDDING TOURISM: MARIJUANA TOURS

On the heels of agritourism is marijuana tourism. Tourists learn about the plant and its uses, visit the places where it is available, and legally sample it as well. Some tours offer lodging and transportation, too. Colorado is not the only state to legalize marijuana. Washington, Oregon, Alaska, and the District of Columbia have also taken steps to legalize the plant.

# CHAPTER 11

# Health and Recreation

Colorado also has a reputation for being a state full of active and athletic people. Besides the famous ski resorts, Colorado offers many other outdoor options for active people. Visitors hit the trails to hike, backpack, and camp. They head to the mountains and national parks to ride their bikes, hunt, and mountain climb. Others take to the water for boating, rafting, and other aquatic fun. Of all money spent by tourists in Colorado, 22 percent comes from outdoor overnight activities. The state is the eighth most popular outdoor destination in the nation. All that healthy outdoor time has created more than 192,000 jobs and pulls in $10 billion for Colorado.

Colorado wants to be the healthiest state in America. It works with public and private health **sectors**. It also collaborates with not-for-profit groups like the Colorado Health Foundation and LiveWell Colorado. Colorado has more

Together, the Fitzsimons Life Science District and the Anschutz Medical Campus make up a property that is 578 acres big! That's 18 million square feet (about 5 million square meters)! It is the country's largest medical improvement project. When it's finished, it will be able to employ more than 30,000 people.

38

*Rock climbing is a popular sport in Colorado, enjoyed by locals and tourists alike.*

than 250,000 people working in health and wellness. Research facilities are expanding, too, such as the Fitzsimons Life Science District and the Anschutz Medical Campus. Here, they do research, educate, and take care of people. The Colorado Health Foundation says, "Healthy Workforce + Healthy Environment = Robust Economy." And with that kind of attitude, the health and economy are bound to keep thriving in this beautiful, exciting state.

In 2013, the Colorado Health Institute started working with the Colorado Office of Economic Development and International Trade (OEDIT) on a specific plan to increase the number of health and wellness jobs and continue growth in the health industry.

# CHAPTER 12

# Oh, the Places We Go: Transportation

Transportation is important everywhere. Colorado is one of the states with the most roads in all the mountain states. Luckily, it has a well-developed transportation system. All different kinds of transportation help out the economy. Goods, or **freight**, are brought from production to the marketplace to be sold by way of air, highways and other roads, rail, and truck. Transportation also includes public transit systems, such as subways. Walking and bicycling are means of transportation. Sidewalks and bicycle lanes help pedestrians and cyclists get around.

Besides being a means to move products, roads and highways are important to the economy. They play a role in local commerce. For example, tourists use highways and local roads to see the state's amazing views. They drive cars, trucks, motorcycles, and more as they sightsee and have fun around the state.

The Colorado Department of Transportation maintains 23,000 total lane miles (37,014 km) of highway.

TRAFFIC GOING TOWARD ROCKY MOUNTAINS

DENVER INTERNATIONAL AIRPORT

The first railroads reached Colorado and the West in the middle-to-late 1800s. This was a big change for the area. It dramatically changed how quickly people and goods could travel from the East Coast of the United States to reach Colorado.

Denver has an international airport. Almost every major airline in the country flies into and out of Denver International Airport (DIA). Denver International Airport boasts North America's longest runway. DIA is also the fifth-busiest airport in the entire country. Airports connect markets all over the world and help them do business with one another. This increases business in Colorado. They bring tourists to Colorado and help people visit and explore the rest of the United States and countries beyond!

Colorado also has many railroads traveling through it. Most of the state's railroads carry goods to and from Colorado. A train can carry a whole lot of products to be bought and sold. Almost all railways are dedicated to carrying products. A rail company called Amtrak also carries people to and from Denver and the Rockies.

UNION STATION IN DOWNTOWN DENVER

# CHAPTER 13

# Services

Much of Colorado's income comes from its service industries. This is the case for most states. But what is a service industry? It is a business that performs some service, or a kind of work, for its customers. Service industries are sometimes called service sectors. The service industry doesn't make a product that other people use. Instead, it provides services people need. People who work in service do something for others. For example, doctors offer medical attention and advice. Teachers educate their students. They teach them what they need to know. Lawyers offer guidance with the law. People working in real estate help their customers buy and sell houses and other property.

In Colorado, the services that top the list are community, business, and personal services. These include private health

## MAJOR MEDICAL

The medical field has a pretty big effect on the economy in Colorado. It has around 253,000 people working in health and wellness throughout the state. These workers account for a $11.3 billion payroll every year.

SKIING AT ARAPAHOE BASIN SKI RESORT

care, ski resorts and hotels, engineering, legal work, and software development. Finance, insurance, and real estate follow up on the services list.

Tourism is the biggest part of the service industry. People who work in tourism guide all those visitors from other states and around the world and help them have a good time. So if you ever have the chance to visit Colorado, just think about how different your visit would be without all those people working in this important part of the economy!

## WALL STREET OF THE WEST

The Front Range area of Colorado is known for its major financial industries. It's one of only a few outside of the northeast. So it has earned the nickname "Wall Street of the West." Service fields in the finance industry include banking and finance, investments, and insurance. Many of those who work in finance help other people manage or invest their money. The city of Denver is an important area for banking and finance.

**45**

# Glossary

**aerospace**—The Earth's skies and space beyond.

**capital**—Wealth, usually money.

**entrepreneur**—One who manages and runs a business, usually with a financial risk.

**freight**—Goods moved from place to place by truck, train, ship, or aircraft.

**hydroelectric**—Using water to create energy.

**industry**—A type or part of economic or commercial activity.

**molybdenum**—A metal used in steel to give it extra strength.

**natural resources**—Materials that occur in nature and can be used to make money.

**millennial**—Someone born in the 1980s or 1990s. Also called Generation Y, or Gen-Yer.

**petroleum**—A liquid that is oily and flammable. It can be made into gasoline, kerosene, and other fuel products.

**production**—Making or manufacturing products, sometimes from natural or raw materials.

**recession**—A period of time when business activity takes a downturn.

**revenue**—Income produced.

**sectors**—A portion of society.

**sole proprietors**—The single owner of a business.

**telecommunications**—The part of technology concerned with communication by telephone, cable, or broadcasting.

# Index

Due to the changing nature of Internet links, the Rosen Publishing Group, Inc., has developed an online list of websites related to the subject of this book. This site is updated regularly. Please use this link to access the list:
http://www.powerkidslinks.com/soco/eoc